There are one hundred an[d] occurring in Europe, includi[ng] as well as the purely terrestr[ial] them have been established [since the Ice] Age about ten thousand y[ears ago. Some] species, such as the Auroch and Tarpan, have died out, others, such as the Brown Rat, the Coypu and the Sika Deer, have been introduced.

In the temperate climate which is enjoyed by almost the whole of Europe, the forests and steppes, the marshlands and mountains provide an ideal habitat for a wide variety of mammals ranging from the tiny Shrew to the huge Wisent. But for thousands of years this enviable habitat has also been attractive to man as perhaps no other part of the globe has been. Great areas of forest, which once covered much of the Continent, have been cleared to provide agricultural land; marshes have been drained, steppes and wild places developed; and cities, with their attendant and inevitable pollution, have been built.

All this has placed an irresistible pressure on the European mammals. Partly from lack of living space and partly from centuries of persecution by man, many have disappeared or are fast disappearing and others have had to adapt to new ways of living. It is essential that those which remain should be intelligently conserved, and that we should learn to share our increasingly crowded living space with them. The pleasure they can give us will be well worth the effort and sacrifices we must make.

A Ladybird Book
Series 691

*'European Mammals' is the fourth of a
Ladybird series of books about animals of
the world. The superb full-colour illustrations
by John Leigh-Pemberton, the well known
bird and animal painter, are supported by an
informative text, and a colourful end-paper
shows the various types of habitat of the
animals. An index is given and also, at
the back, a chart showing the various Orders
and Families to which the animals belong.*

A Ladybird
'ANIMALS OF THE WORLD' Book

EUROPEAN MAMMALS

written and illustrated by
JOHN LEIGH-PEMBERTON

Publishers: Ladybird Books Ltd . Loughborough
© Ladybird Books Ltd (formerly Wills & Hepworth Ltd) 1971
Printed in England

Hedgehog (*above*)	Length, head and body	25 cm.
	Length of tail	3 cm.
Mole (*below*)	Length, head and body	13·5 cm.
	Length of tail	3 cm.

Hedgehogs (order *Insectivora*, family *Erinaceidae*) are found throughout Europe with the exception of Iceland and northern Scandinavia. Chiefly nocturnal, they protect themselves from danger by rolling into a ball and presenting an array of needle-sharp spines with which the whole upper part of the body is covered. Two litters of four young, blind and with soft, white spines, are produced each year.

In the colder parts of their range, Hedgehogs go into partial hibernation in winter, building a leafy nest in which to do so. They make sounds ranging from grunts to wails and they very easily become tame. They are almost entirely insectivorous.

In southern Spain and the Balearic Islands occurs the Vagrant Hedgehog, common throughout Africa.

Two species of Mole (order *Insectivora*, family *Talpidae*) are distributed throughout Europe, although they are not found in Ireland, Iceland, or in the northern parts of Scandinavia. The Common Mole is replaced in parts of Spain and Greece by the Blind Mole, the habits of both species being similar. Living almost entirely underground, moles construct complex systems of tunnels and chambers, from a few centimetres to about 60 cm. below the surface. For this they use powerful and specially adapted fore-limbs. Excavated soil appears above the surface as mole hills.

Moles are not entirely blind, but their small eyes are usually hidden by their velvety fur. One litter a year of about four young is usual.

Moles squeak or, during their frequent fights, utter a shrill, twittering cry. Their diet consists almost entirely of earthworms and larvae.

 0 7214 0283 6

Common Shrew (top right)	Length, head and body	7·5 cm.
Pygmy Shrew (top left)	Length, head and body	5·5 cm.
White-toothed Shrew (lower left)	Length, head and body	8 cm.
Savi's Pygmy Shrew or Etruscan Shrew (centre left)	Length, head and body / Weight	4·5 cm. / 2 gr.
Water Shrew (bottom right)	Length, head and body / Weight	8·5 cm. / 12 gr.

The order *Insectivora* consists chiefly of the family *Soricidae*, the Shrews. There are two hundred and sixty five species in the world, eleven of which are found throughout Europe, with the exception of Iceland.

Shrews occupy a variety of habitats from marsh to mountains and are insectivorous and carnivorous; they have enormous appetites and are born with a complete set of teeth. They are bad-tempered and whenever they meet they fight or indulge in screaming matches. Having such minute bones, thin as bristles, they are easily injured fatally, and are also very prone to die of fright. The average life-span is no more than eighteen months. They do not hibernate and are active by day and night. Several litters a year are born, consisting of from two to ten young.

The Common Shrew, absent from Ireland and Spain, is found elsewhere throughout Europe. Ireland has the Pygmy Shrew which is also found throughout Europe, but perhaps less commonly. In Spain its place is taken by the White-toothed Shrew, found in other countries of western Europe but not in Britain or Scandinavia.

Savi's Pygmy Shrew or Etruscan Shrew is the smallest mammal in the world. It is found in Spain, the Mediterranean coast, Italy and Greece and is rather rare.

The Water Shrew spends much time under water, catching small fish, frogs and insects. It is found all over Europe, but not in Spain or Ireland.

6

Brown Hare (*above*)	Length, head and body	55 cm.
	Length of tail	10·5 cm.
	Weight	3·5 Kg.
Rabbit (*below*)	Length, head and body	40 cm.
	Length of tail	6 cm.
	Weight	1·75 Kg.

Hares and Rabbits are placed in the order *Lagomorpha*, family *Leporidae*. They are both vegetarian and active by night and, to a lesser extent, by day. The young of Rabbits are born naked, blind and helpless, usually in an underground burrow; those of Hares are born with eyes open, fully furred, in a nest or 'form' above ground. Both species scream when hurt or frightened but are otherwise rather silent; both depend on speed for protection and have acute senses of smell and hearing.

The Brown Hare is found everywhere in Europe, except in Iceland, Norway and in parts of Ireland, in which countries it is replaced by the Blue Hare. Flat, cultivated land is the preferred habitat, but moors and woodland are also favoured. Two or three litters of three or four young are produced yearly.

Usually solitary, except during a spectacular mating period, Hares have a home territory, every centimetre of which they know intimately.

Rabbits probably originated in Spain and southern France, but have spread to other western European countries or have been introduced, as in Britain, for their value as food and fur producers. They are a major pest to agriculture but in many places their numbers have recently been much reduced by disease. They construct extensive 'warrens' or systems of burrows and produce as many as six litters of about six young each year.

Black or silvery Rabbits occur quite commonly in some areas, and many varieties of Domestic Rabbits have been derived from the wild form.

Edible Dormouse (*bottom*)	Length, head and body	16 cm.
	Length of tail	13 cm.
Garden Dormouse (*middle left*)	Length, head and body	13 cm.
	Length of tail	10·5 cm.
Forest Dormouse (*middle right*)	Length, head and body	10 cm.
	Length of tail	8·5 cm.
Common Dormouse (*top*)	Length, head and body	7·5 cm.
	Length of tail	6·5 cm.

Five species of Dormouse (order *Rodentia*, family *Gliridae*) occur in Europe. All are nocturnal (as indicated by their large eyes), extremely good climbers (as indicated by their hands and 'balancing' tails), and all of them hibernate. They are vegetarian, eating fruit and nuts, but will also take insects and sometimes eggs and young birds. Dormice usually have one litter a year of from two to nine young, and for breeding and hibernation they make nests of grass and moss, placed in a tree, a cavity or even in the roofs of houses.

The Edible Dormouse is so called because the Romans bred it as a table delicacy, fattening it on chestnuts in special jars. It is found from the Pyrenees eastward across Europe and down to the Mediterranean. It is absent from the more northerly parts of Europe, but has been introduced into Britain (1902, Hertfordshire) and is still established there, often—during hibernation—in houses.

The Garden Dormouse occupies roughly the same area but extends also into Spain and northern France and even into the Gulf of Finland. It is rather noisy, snoring, whistling, squeaking and growling.

The Forest Dormouse is found in south-eastern Europe, as also is the very rare Ognev's Dormouse (not shown) which is really an Asiatic species.

The Common Dormouse or Hazel Mouse is found throughout Europe except in Spain and Scandinavia. It still occurs in parts of England but is becoming rarer. It was at one time much kept as a pet, but being nocturnal is rather dull although extremely pretty.

Bank Vole (*centre*)	Length, head and body	10 cm.
	Length of tail	5 cm.
Harvest Mouse (*above*)	Length, head and body	7 cm.
	Length of tail	6 cm.
Wood Mouse (*below*)	Length, head and body	9 cm.
(Field Mouse)	Length of tail	9 cm.

The family *Cricetidae* (order *Rodentia*) includes the Voles, of which there are fourteen European species, three species of European Lemmings, three species of Hamster and the Muskrat*, a species introduced from North America.

Voles are blunt-nosed, mainly nocturnal and vegetarian. They occupy a variety of habitats from streams to mountains. Many species make tunnels in grass or in the litter of woodland, and the numbers of all of them tend to fluctuate with population explosions and declines. They provide the principle food source for many predators.

One of the commonest Voles is the Bank Vole, found throughout much of Europe. Whenever it is absent it is replaced by a similar species, except in Iceland and Ireland. Four or five litters of about five young are born each season.

Europe contains about nine species of the family *Muridae* (order *Rodentia*), the old world Rats and Mice. The smallest of these is the Harvest Mouse, found from the Pyrenees eastward, but not in Ireland, Iceland, Scandinavia or southern Mediterranean countries. These mice, which have partly prehensile tails, make nests around stems of grass or crops and raise several families of about five young. Diet is of vegetable and some insect material; the voice is a quiet chirrup and there is no hibernation.

Four types of Field Mouse occupy between them nearly all Europe except the most northerly parts. One of the widest spread is the Wood Mouse which lives chiefly in grassland. Breeding occurs throughout the year, families consisting of about five young. Seeds, fruit, ants, insects and snails are eaten. They do not hibernate.

See also 'North American Mammals' in this series.

Black Rat (*centre*)	*Length, head and body*	*19 cm.*
	Length of tail	*21 cm.*
Brown Rat (*above*)	*Length, head and body*	*25 cm.*
	Length of tail	*20 cm.*
House Mouse (*below*)	*Length, head and body*	*8·5 cm.*
	Length of tail	*8·5 cm.*

These three animals are members of the family *Muridae* (order *Rodentia*) and, in Europe, all are more or less dependant for their living on Man and are 'parasites'. They are more widely spread in Europe than any other mammal and at least two of them occur even in Iceland. They are serious pests, very difficult to control, and do an immense amount of damage as well as spreading diseases. Omnivorous and mainly nocturnal, they are inquisitive, cautious, cunning and adaptable.

The Black Rat, Asiatic in origin, reached Europe in ships by the thirteenth century and brought with it the fleas which caused plagues such as the Black Death. It is a good climber and usually occupies the higher stories of buildings, breeding throughout the year and producing about eight young in each litter. In Europe it has to a great extent been replaced by the larger Brown Rat which originated in China and reached Europe in the sixteenth and Britain in the eighteenth century. Unlike the Black Rat, it digs burrows and can live on farmland as well as in the lower parts of buildings. Breeding is much the same as the Black Rat and colour in both species varies considerably.

The House Mouse is even more widely spread and occurs in several forms, some living in woodland or on farmland, as well as in houses. They breed throughout the year, litters averaging five young each and they provide a food source for nearly all predators, particularly Barn Owls. The voice is a high, frequently-uttered squeak.

Crested Porcupine
(below)

Length, head and body	65 cm.
Length of tail	10 cm.

Pine Marten *(above)*

Length, head and body	48 cm.
Length of tail	24 cm.

The Crested Porcupine is a large rodent (family *Hystricidae*) which may have been introduced into Europe in Roman times. It now exists in limited numbers on the western slopes of the Apennines in Italy, in Sicily and in northern Greece. These nocturnal animals are mostly vegetarian, but will eat carrion and are reputed to gnaw bones. They live in burrows and defend themselves by turning their backs to an enemy, raising their quills and running backwards towards him. These quills are of varying lengths (up to 40 cm.), are hollow and rattle when erected.

There are two litters each year of three or four young which, like all Porcupines, are highly developed at birth and arrive equipped with soft spines which quickly harden. This species and others similar are also found through most of Africa and in Asia.

The Pine Marten is found through most of Europe but is everywhere decreasing. Rare in the British Isles (where it is making a partial recovery) it is absent from Spain and Greece, although in these two countries the somewhat similar Beech Marten occurs.

This inhabitant of woodland is a *Carnivore* (family *Mustelidae*) and a wonderfully agile and graceful climber which nests in hollow trees or old birds' nests or in rock cavities. It is chiefly active at dusk but is otherwise nocturnal and lives on rodents, small birds, some insects, fish and berries. Three young, very pale in colour, are born each year and there is only one litter. The voice ranges from growls and squeaks to a peculiar and characteristic call note 'tok-tok-tok'.

*Wolf

Length, head and body	125 cm.
Length of tail	35 cm.
Shoulder height	75 cm.
Weight	40 Kg.

Wolves (order *Carnivora*, family *Canidae*) were fairly common in Europe until about the seventeenth century. Since then, because they killed domestic animals, they have been much persecuted and in some places, such as Britain, totally exterminated. Apart from Bears they are the largest predatory carnivores in Europe and are most useful in helping to control the numbers of sick and aged grazing animals such as deer and in keeping down large populations of such animal pests as rabbits, rodents and even insects.

Wolves are still found in Spain and Portugal, in Italy, the Balkan countries, Russia and Scandinavia. They are very hardy and intelligent and can adapt to any sort of habitat, from woodland to mountain, which affords them a source of food. They wander enormous distances, often solitary, sometimes in family parties, and occasionally, in winter, in packs. Generally speaking, solitary Wolves hunt smaller prey and only a pack will seek out larger animals.

A single litter of four or five cubs (thirteen have been recorded) is raised each year, and Wolves, which are believed to mate for life, are particularly good parents. They bark rather rarely and somewhat like a dog and have a distinctive howl, normally heard from October to December.

It is usually assumed that all breeds of Domestic Dog are descended from the various forms of Wolves which occur throughout the northern hemisphere, and that possibly Jackals also contributed to the Dog's ancestry. The Dog's origins go back at least eight thousand years and it is unlikely that we shall ever know exactly how Dogs started.

See also 'North American Mammals' *in this series.*

Fox (*above*)	Length, head and body	65 cm.
	Length of tail	40 cm.
Red Squirrel (*below*)	Length, head and body	22 cm.
	Length of tail	18 cm.

Foxes (order *Carnivora*, family *Canidae*) are found in every country in Europe except in Iceland and Crete. They occur in two forms, the Common Fox and the Brant or Cross Fox which has a dark mask, neck and underside.

In spite of centuries of persecution, the intelligence, wariness, hardiness and adaptability of the Fox have enabled it to survive in almost any habitat. Foxes eat a wide variety of foods from blackberries to hares, but the greater part of their diet consists of rabbits and voles, thus probably doing much more good than harm.

One litter of four or five cubs are born in a large burrow or 'earth' each year. They are raised and 'educated' by the female (Vixen) while the male (Dog Fox) supplies much of the food. Foxes have a shrill bark and a characteristic 'scream' during the breeding season.

The Red Squirrel (order *Rodentia*, family *Sciuridae*) occurs throughout Europe but is absent from some islands. This is a woodland animal, active during the day and living almost entirely in the trees. It does not hibernate. A large nest ('drey'), built of twigs and lined with moss, is used as living quarters and one or two families of about three young are raised each year.

Squirrels change their coats twice a year, the ears and tails once a year and, in summer, the tail is almost white. Food, often buried for future use (but often abandoned), consists almost entirely of seeds and nuts although birds' eggs are also taken. The voice is an angry chatter.

Arctic Fox
    (*two forms, above*)
Norway Lemming
    (*below*)

Length, head and body   55 cm.
Length of tail   30 cm.

Length, head and body   14 cm.

Arctic Foxes (order *Carnivora*, family *Canidae*) live in mountains, on tundra or ice floes and on the seashore around the Arctic region. In Europe they are found in Iceland and northern Scandinavia and, like most Arctic mammals, they do not hibernate. The thick, white, winter coat which they wear from October to April enables them to stand temperatures well below minus 50°C. The summer coat is much thinner and is brown. There is a 'Blue' form of this fox, in which the coat is grey-brown throughout the year. One litter of about eight pups is born in May or June each year.

Baby seals, whale carcasses, carrion and the kills of Polar Bears* are included in the diet, and food is stored for the winter near burrows which are dug into a cliff face or into a bank of snow. The principal food-source is the Lemming, the availability of which determines the Arctic Fox population.

Norway Lemmings (order *Rodentia*, family *Cricetidae*) inhabit mountains in northern Scandinavia, where they live in tunnels dug beneath the moss or under snow. Nocturnal, aggressive and vegetarian, Lemmings are subject to great expansions in population about every three or four years. At these times they migrate in swarms in search of food, allowing nothing to check them; eventually large numbers reach the sea and plunge in, swimming until they drown. They leave virtually no vegetation behind them, endangering the livelihood of many other species.

Several litters of about six young are born each year in a spherical nest made of moss.

See also 'North American Mammals' *in this series.*

Weasel (*centre*)	*Length, head and body*	20 cm.
	Length of tail	6 cm.
	(Females much smaller)	
Stoat (*winter, above summer, below*)	*Length, head and body*	28 cm.
	Length of tail	10 cm.
	(Females smaller)	

Stoats and Weasels belong to the order *Carnivora*, family *Mustelidae*, and are among the most efficient predators in the world. Weasels are found throughout Europe with the exception of Ireland and some islands, the Stoat being present in Ireland but absent from Spain and southern Europe.

Weasels live in a variety of dry habitats and are often found near farm buildings, searching ricks for mice in their holes. They are mostly nocturnal and live principally on small rodents; but they are sufficiently efficient as killers to tackle young rabbits, birds and poultry. Prey is killed, as with most of the *Mustelidae*, by a bite through the back of the neck. Two litters of 'kittens' are born each year, the numbers varying between four and eleven.

Stoats can be distinguished from Weasels by their greater size and by the black tip to their tails. In winter in some parts of their range they turn white and are then known as Ermine. They prefer woodland habitats and are active by day and night, climbing and swimming more expertly than the Weasel and being more inclined to live and hunt in family parties.

When hunting, Stoats perform a series of acrobatics which seems to have the effect of fascinating their prey—chiefly the rabbit. There is usually one litter a year, the kittens being white.

Both these species have been ruthlessly persecuted by farmers and gamekeepers; this is a great mistake, for in killing rabbits and rodents they do an immense amount of good.

Otter (*above*)	Length, head and body	75 cm.
	Length of tail	45 cm.
Water Vole (*below*)	Length, head and body	20 cm.
	Length of tail	12·5 cm.

Iceland, Corsica and Sardinia are the only sizeable parts of Europe from which the Otter is absent. It is an animal of streams, rivers and lakes, although quite often found in coastal waters and even some way from water. It belongs to the order *Carnivora*, family *Mustelidae*, and has webbed feet and a powerful tail which is its chief instrument of propulsion in the water. It can stay submerged for about seven minutes and lives on shellfish, fish, frogs, some mammals, but chiefly upon eels.

Otters are mainly nocturnal and live singly or in family parties which are very playful, making 'slides' in mud or snow. The nest, or 'holt' is in the bank of a stream or in a hollow tree, and one litter of two or three cubs is raised each year. Cubs have a distinctive piping cry which in the adult animal becomes a short whistle, but generally Otters are fairly silent.

Otters are hunted quite needlessly, as they do little harm and much good to river life; in parts of Europe they are trapped for their fur. They are becoming scarcer, increasingly so because many rivers are now polluted.

The Water Vole (order *Rodentia*, family *Cricetidae*) is found in streams in Britain (apart from Ireland) and in France and Spain. Elsewhere it is replaced by the Ground Vole.

It makes burrows in stream banks with an underwater entrance, and special breeding nests among reeds, where several litters are raised each year. Food is almost entirely vegetable with a few mussels and snails. It is an expert swimmer, active day and night.

Reindeer (*above*)	Length, head and body	200 cm.
	Length of tail	15 cm.
	Shoulder height	115 cm.
Wild Cat (*below*)	Length, head and body	65 cm.
	Length of tail	35 cm.

In Europe, Reindeer (order *Artiodactyla*, family *Cervidae*) are found in Lappland, Russia and Iceland and on other islands within the Arctic Circle. They have also been experimentally introduced into Scotland in recent years. According to locality they vary tremendously in colour and size and many are kept in herds as domestic animals, yielding meat, milk, hides and hair. Both stags and hinds carry antlers and have broad hooves which make a clicking sound as they walk. Herds migrate in winter in search of food, which consists chiefly of moss, for which Reindeer will dig through snow. One, or sometimes two unspotted young are born each year.

The Wild Cats of Europe occur in several forms and in isolated areas from Scotland southwards and eastwards across Europe. Parts of Europe have African species and others, such as Scandinavia, no Wild Cats at all. In Scotland particularly there has been much interbreeding with Domestic Cats, although it is unlikely that the latter are descended from the European Wild Cat.

This exceptionally fierce, untameable animal (order *Carnivora*, family *Felidae*) lives in remote woodland and mountain habitats and is principally nocturnal. Food includes birds, fish and large insects as well as Blue Hares, rabbits, young deer or lambs. Prey is ambushed or stalked and often the head is removed.

Two to four kittens are born each year in a well concealed den, and sometimes there is a second or third litter. The family's home territory is defended by the male, the kittens being reared by the female alone, as the male sometimes kills them.

See also as Caribou in 'North American Mammals' in this series.

Genet (above)	Length, head and body	54 cm.
	Length of tail	45 cm.
Spanish Lynx (below)	Length, head and body	100 cm.
	Length of tail	12·5 cm.

The Genet (order *Carnivora*, family *Viverridae*) is a rather unexpected animal to find among European fauna. Similar to the species common in Africa it is found in Spain, Portugal and western France. This shy, nocturnal and rarely seen creature has retractile claws, similar to those of the Cats, and the musky smell typical of this family. It lives among rocks in dense woodland, usually near streams, and lives on small mammals, birds and some insects. It is an excellent climber.

Two or three young are born in two litters each year, and for so small an animal the life span is fairly long, probably ten years. European Genets are usually greyer in colour than those of Africa, and are related to the Mongoose, another mammal which occurs in southwest Spain, and to the Civets.

Spain is also the home of the Spanish Lynx (order *Carnivora*, family *Felidae*), a rare relative of the Northern Lynx and bearing the same relationship to it as the Bobcat does to the Canadian Lynx in North America.* Brighter in colour, smaller and more densely spotted than the Northern Lynx, this is a mountain and woodland animal living principally on rabbits and birds. It has been much persecuted in the past and like all Lynxes is becoming scarcer, although, thanks largely to the efforts of the World Wildlife Fund, it is now effectively protected in at least part of its range.

Breeding and other habits are similar to those of other Lynxes and, like them, it is normally solitary, with exceptional senses of smell and eyesight.

*See also 'North American Mammals' *in this series*

Polecat (*below*)

Length, head and body	40 cm.
Length of tail	18 cm.
(*Females smaller*)	

Wild Boar (*above*)

Length, head and body	140 cm.
Length of tail	18 cm.
Weight (*Boar*)	170 Kg.
(*The Sow is smaller and lighter*)	

Many mammals, particularly members of the families *Mustelidae* and *Viverridae*, have glands situated beneath the tail which can emit a characteristic and often highly offensive smell. The Skunk* is a good example of this and the Polecat (order *Carnivora*, family *Mustelidae*) is another.

Polecats are found in two forms, varying in colour, throughout Europe, although they are now rare in Britain and are absent from Scandinavia, Ireland, Iceland and the most southerly parts of Europe. In extreme south-east Europe another species, the Marbled Polecat, occurs.

In many ways Polecats are similar to Stoats, of which they are a larger version. They tend naturally to take larger prey and include eels in their diet, but live principally on rabbits. Although they are found in many habitats, they seem to prefer dense woodland or rocky areas of mountains. Two litters of four or five young are produced each year. Unfortunately they have for long been classed as vermin and have been much persecuted.

Wild Boar (order *Artiodactyla*, family *Suidae*) are found in much of Europe from Portugal to the Balkans, but are absent from all the northern countries and from Alpine regions. They inhabit woodland and farmland and are nocturnal and mainly vegetarian, living in small herds and travelling great distances in search of food. They spend much time wallowing in mud but are extremely active, running and swimming much better than their shape might suggest. When angry they are very dangerous.

As many as twelve piglets, which are striped, are born in a litter. Our Domestic Pigs are derived from this animal.

32   *See also 'North American Mammals' in this series.*

Red Deer

Length, head and body 165–250 cm.
Length of tail   12–15 cm.
Shoulder height   105–140 cm.
Weight   95–250 Kg.
Antlers about 100 cm. in length.
(Hinds smaller and lighter)

Although found in most European countries, Red Deer (order *Artiodactyla*, family *Cervidae*) live in separated 'pockets' and do not form a continuous population across the Continent. They do not occur in Iceland, Sicily or southern Italy and the densest population is in eastern Europe. Nearly everywhere they are woodland animals but in Scotland have completely adapted to living on moorland and mountains.

All modern Red Deer are smaller than their ancestors of the distant past, which were enormous and had massive antlers. To-day, the deer of eastern Europe are the largest and those found in Scotland and Holland the smallest. They are shot or hunted wherever they occur.

Red Deer live in herds, the composition of which varies with the time of year. During the autumn mating season (the 'rut') groups of hinds are collected by a mature stag; in summer and winter there are sometimes mixed herds but separated herds of stags and hinds are formed in spring. Old stags are usually solitary, and sometimes a mixed herd will be led by an old hind. During the 'rut' much fighting takes place between the stags; this is occasionally fatal, but is really more a trial of strength—the winner possessing the hinds.

Various sorts of vegetation are eaten, even seaweed, and Red Deer undoubtedly damage crops. They bark when alarmed, and during the 'rut' the stags roar challenges ('belling') to each other.

Only the stags have antlers, usually cast (and often eaten) in March and fully grown again by July. A single spotted calf is born in May or June.

Wisent
(European Bison)

Length, head and body	270 cm.
Length of tail	80 cm.
Shoulder height	190 cm.
Weight	850 Kg. or more

The Wisent (order *Artiodactyla*, family *Bovidae*) is the largest European land mammal and affords an example of how intelligent conservation can rescue a species from extinction.

From the seventeenth century onwards the numbers of this huge animal, which once inhabited much of the Continent, have rapidly decreased. This has been due partly to hunting and also because of the destruction of the forest and woodland habitat. There were two forms—the large, lowland form and the lighter, mountain form which came from the Caucasus and, apart from one bull, became extinct at the beginning of the present century.

By 1923 there were fifty-six animals of the lowland Wisent left, all in zoos. A society formed for the Wisents' protection collected them together and bred from them, so that to-day the numbers have increased to over eight hundred, of which more than a hundred have been established in the wild in the Bialowieza National Park in Poland. Attempts have also been made to 'reconstitute' the mountain Wisent from the cross-bred stock descended from the sole survivor.

Wisent are browsers, needing large areas of undisturbed woodland. The small herds are active in early morning and evening. Both bulls and the considerably smaller cows have horns, and calves, usually born singly in May or June, take about eight years to become fully grown.

Longer in the leg than the American Bison*, Wisents hold their heads higher. The two species have been interbred and characteristics of behaviour, such as wallowing, are common to both.

Both species need protection in order to survive.

*See also 'North American Mammals' *in this series.*

Elk (*above*)	Length, head and body	250 cm.
	Shoulder height	200 cm.
	Weight	400 Kg.
	(*Females considerably smaller*)	
Brown Bear (*below*)	Length, head and body	200 cm.
	Shoulder height	100 cm.
	Weight	200 Kg.

Elk* (order *Artiodactyla*, family *Cervidae*) are referred to as Moose in North America, where the word 'Elk' is wrongly applied to the Wapiti. This is the largest deer in the world and occurs in fair numbers throughout Scandinavia and in Russia. At the present time it is spreading southward and westward in Europe.

In summer, Elk favour marshy or lakeland habitats, often entering the water and feeding on water plants. In winter the protection of drier woodland areas is preferred. Elk do not form herds and are solitary, except during the 'rut'. They are chiefly browsers and are, to a large extent, nocturnal. Calves, unspotted, are born singly and stay with the mother for up to two years.

The European form of the Brown Bear (order *Carnivora*, family *Ursidae*) is a woodland and mountain animal which once occurred all over Europe but which is now rapidly becoming scarcer. There are Bears in parts of Spain, in Greece, in Scandinavia, Russia and a few parts of eastern Europe, but in many places only a few individuals exist and do not form a secure breeding stock.

The Bear is the largest European carnivore, mainly nocturnal and nearly always solitary. Some individuals are vegetarian, some omnivorous and others flesh-eaters. They are intensely inquisitive with a remarkably developed sense of smell and very poor eyesight. Brown Bears do not climb trees but swim well and wander over large areas. There is a long resting period during the winter, not true hibernation, during which one to three very small cubs are born.

*See also 'North American Mammals' *in this series.*

Fallow Deer (*above*)	Length, head and body	145 cm.
	Length of tail	17 cm.
	Shoulder height	100 cm.
Badger (*below*)	Length, head and body	70 cm.
	Length of tail	17 cm.
	Weight	20 Kg.

Fallow Deer (order *Artiodactyla*, family *Cervidae*) probably originated in southern Europe and Asia Minor. But many centuries ago they spread or were deliberately introduced into much of western Europe and are now established there in woodland habitats. They are not found in northern Scandinavia and are rare in Italy and Spain. Many are kept in parks, especially in Britain, where they were well established in Norman times.

The bucks have flattened ('palmated') antlers, cast in April and fully grown again by August. As with all deer, the antlers, while growing, have a 'velvet' skin and are very sensitive until they have hardened and the velvet has rubbed off. Does (females) do not have antlers and during most of the year form separate herds. The 'rut' takes place in October and the fawns, usually single, are born in May or June.

Fallow Deer are grazers, but also eat the bark of trees.

Badgers (order *Carnivora*, family *Mustelidae*) are found throughout Europe except for Iceland and northern Scandinavia. Almost entirely nocturnal, they live on rabbits and rodents, but also eat many earthworms, wasps and acorns. They live in family groups in burrows ('sets') which are complex tunnel systems with chambers for sleeping and breeding. Nesting material such as bracken is regularly taken outside and 'aired' on sunny days. They are particularly attractive animals which do a great deal of good.

From one to five cubs are born each year and there is only one litter. In Poland, Scandinavia and Russia the Badger hibernates but elsewhere is active throughout the year.

Roe Deer (*below*)	Length, head and body	120 cm.
	Length of tail	3 cm.
	Shoulder height	70 cm.
Grey Squirrel (*above*)	Length, head and body	26 cm.
	Length of tail	21·5 cm.

Roe Deer (order *Artiodactyla*, family *Cervidae*) differ in many respects from other members of this family. They do not form large herds, but each family group of Roe Deer has its own territory, where boundaries are established by 'fraying' trees and by depositing scent. Well defined rings marked out on the ground round a bush or similar object are made by the buck chasing the doe during the 'rut' in late summer. The spotted young are born in May, twins being frequent and triplets not uncommon.

Secretive, mainly nocturnal and with a distinctive deep bark, these Deer, which are browsers, are found in most of Europe but not in Iceland, Ireland and some islands. They prefer woodland but are sometimes found on mountain slopes. The small antlers, shed in November and re-grown by May, are carried by the buck only and in winter the red summer coat changes to grey.

Other Deer species found in Europe are the results of introduction or escapes from zoos. These include the Japanese Sika, established in Britain, France, Germany and Denmark, and the Chinese Muntjac and Chinese Water Deer living wild in England and France.

Between 1876 and 1929 the American Eastern Grey Squirrel (order *Rodentia*, family *Sciuridae*) was introduced into England and since that date has spread to many other areas in Britain. It is not found elsewhere in Europe but in Britain has largely taken the place of the Red Squirrel (which was already declining there). It inhabits gardens and town parks as well as woodland, raising two families a year.

Northern Lynx (*below*)	Length, head and body	100 cm.
	Length of tail	18 cm.
	Shoulder height	70 cm.
Saiga (*above*)	Length, head and body	130 cm.
	Length of tail	9 cm.
	Shoulder height	76 cm.

The range of the Northern Lynx, a close relative of the Canadian Lynx*, is from Norway, across Scandinavia and eastern Europe to western Asia. It was once more wide-spread but like all Lynxes (order *Carnivora*, family *Felidae*) is becoming scarcer and is increasingly being driven to isolated areas far from its only enemy—Man. But, curiously, at times Lynx will appear in places where they have not been seen for years, and it is to be hoped that they will be protected and be able to re-establish themselves.

Prey consists of animals from Deer down to small rodents, hunted chiefly at night, but the principal food source is the Blue Hare. When these are scarce, the Lynx has to wander far afield.

Three young are born in a hollow tree or rock cavity and there is only one litter.

The only antelope native to Europe is the Saiga (order *Artiodactyla*, family *Bovidae*) found in Kazakhstan, between the Don and Volga rivers and into Asia. Once existing in gigantic herds across the Russian Steppes, the Saiga became almost extinct in Europe during the severe winter of 1829. It is now returning and very sensibly is protected.

The extraordinary 'inflated' nose contains structures found elsewhere only in some whales and its function is to warm the air and to filter dust from it.

Bucks do not feed during the November 'rut' and in consequence many of them do not survive the winter. Calves are born in May during the annual northerly migration of the herds.

44   *See also* 'North American Mammals' *in this series.*

Blue Hare (below)

Length, head and body	58 cm.
Length of tail	6 cm.
(Smaller in some areas)	

Wolverine (above)

Length, head and body	80 cm.
Length of tail	14 cm.
Shoulder height	42 cm.

The Blue Hare (order *Lagomorpha*, family *Leporidae*) is found in the most northerly parts of Europe and in the Alps. It is one of the few mammals found in Iceland and occurs all over Ireland, another country with a very limited fauna.

Smaller than the Brown Hare and with shorter ears, the Blue Hare usually turns white in winter. It is an animal of woods and mountains (up to about 1200 metres) in summer and is related to the Canadian Snowshoe Hare*. Two or three young are born in each of two or three litters in most years, but the numbers fluctuate greatly, probably according to the supply of food which consists largely of heather.

Blue Hares are very extensively preyed upon by Eagles, Foxes, Stoats and Wild Cats.

The Wolverine (order *Carnivora*, family *Mustelidae*) is one of the toughest, fiercest animals on earth, avoided by other predators and able to kill quite large deer. Immensely strong, it travels more readily over snow than other animals and is thus able to hunt them down. Other food eaten includes berries, birds and their eggs and carrion.

Wolverines are rarely seen and nowhere common, but their range extends right round the Arctic Circle and they inhabit moorland, marsh and forest. In Europe they are found in Norway, Sweden, Finland and Russia. Each animal, particularly the male, requires a large territory and mature males usually have two or three mates. Two or three young are born in February in a den, and because they mature rather slowly there is only one litter a year.

46   *See also 'North American Mammals' in this series.

Chamois (*above*)

Length, head and body	*120 cm.*
Length of tail	*4 cm.*
Shoulder height	*75 cm.*

Mouflon (*below*)

Length, head and body	*120 cm.*
Length of tail	*5 cm.*
Shoulder height	*70 cm.*
Length of horns	*76 cm.*

Chamois (order *Artiodactyla*, family *Bovidae*) are 'goat-antelopes' which inhabit mountainous woodland up to 2300 metres. They occur in the Pyrenees, the Alps, the Apennines, the Carpathians and in the Balkans. In some places they have been almost exterminated by uncontrolled hunting, but are becoming re-established as a result of protection.

Wonderfully agile climbers and jumpers, Chamois can live in inaccessible places and are also extremely wary. The small bands, always led by a female, have sentries which give warning of approaching danger.Food consists of grass, leaves and flowers and Chamois are active during the day. Both sexes carry horns and live for as many as twenty years.

One or two kids are born annually and within a few days of birth can jump and climb with their mother. Should a kid become orphaned the whole herd takes care of it—a rather unusual characteristic among mammals.

Mouflon (order *Artiodactyla*, family *Bovidae*) are mountain sheep, occupying heights at the level of the tree line and coming originally from Corsica and Sardinia. From here they have been introduced into mountain areas in other parts of Europe, particularly eastern Europe.

This is not a common animal and is becoming rarer—the magnificent horns of the ram being unfortunately much prized by hunters. Like all sheep they are grazers, feeding only at dusk and hiding during the day. They are similar in many aspects to the Bighorn Sheep* of North America.

The 'rut' takes place, with much fighting, in September, and one or two lambs are born each year.

48   *See also ' North American Mammals' *in this series.*

Ibex (*above*)

Length, head and body	*140 cm.*
Length of tail	*14 cm.*
Shoulder height	*72 cm.*

Alpine Marmot (*below*)

Length, head and body	*54 cm.*
Length of tail	*15 cm.*

The numbers of Ibex (order *Artiodactyla*, family *Bovidae*), Chamois and Mouflon have all suffered serious decline. It was once believed that parts of them, such as the heart and the stomach stones or bezoars (which many goats and sheep create) were of great medicinal value. As a result, poachers almost exterminated them by the middle of the nineteenth century.

The Ibex, practically extinct, was only saved by the creation of the Gran Paradiso Reserve in the Italian Alps. From this stock are descended the other Ibex found elsewhere in Europe. On some islands, such as Crete, similar species still precariously exist in the wild.

Both sexes carry horns, those of the male being immense. These animals live in high mountains up to 3000 metres, produce single kids and are both browsers and grazers.

Also found in the high mountains of the Alps is the Alpine Marmot (order *Rodentia*, family *Sciuridae*), a large relative of the Squirrel which lives in colonies in complicated burrow systems. They are very active in daylight and frequently sit bolt upright to keep watch for predators such as Eagles. They are quite powerful animals, capable of defending themselves against a fox. Four or five young are produced in spring.

Up to eight months of the year are spent in a hibernation so deep that the body temperature drops to 4°C and it is impossible to wake them.